What's Right with This Picture?

Teaching Kids Character Strengths Through Stories

Chief Storyteller: Renee Jain

Professional Doodler: Nikki Abramowitz

Contents

Introduction for Parents and Teachers

Social and Emotional Learning Revolutionized

"We must remember that intelligence is not enough. Intelligence plus character—that is the goal of true education."

-Martin Luther King Jr.

Why ask what's right with this picture?

Searching for "what's wrong" in any situation comes naturally to most people. In fact, detecting and dwelling on the negative is part of intelligent human design. Think about cavemen who went out gathering food for their families. Those who survived did so because they were sharply attuned to attacks from saber-toothed cats lurking in the bush. In modern times, we don't have a regular need to run from predators, yet we have retained an evolutionary imprint coined the negativity bias.

The negativity bias is a tendency to have greater sensitivity to negative than to positive events or circumstance. Some researchers suggest that, psychologically, negative events carry nearly three times more weight than positive events! This makes it easy for us to hone in on and ruminate on the bad stuff around us. Although this bias may serve us well in situations related to survival, it can have detrimental consequences in modern life.

One of these consequences may be our relentless focus on rooting out and fixing weaknesses in those we love—especially when it comes to our children (e.g., don't eat that, study harder, spend more time with Grandma! etc.). All of this, of course, is in the interest of increasing their well-being. After all, we just want the best for our kids. Yet, what if figuring out "what's wrong" and fixing it is only half the equation to living a good life? It turns out that the research supports this conclusion.

In fact, helping our kids to identify and apply "what's right" or their greatest strengths can not only increase their well-being, but can help drive them toward personal and professional life success. Let's take a look at some of the research.

The research

The research is clear: identifying and applying character strengths increases life satisfaction and well-being. Mounds of research supports this link between character strengths and life satisfaction. And a recent study even reveals that more than just a link, practicing character strengths triggers an increase in one's sense of well-being.

As it relates to youth, here are just a few specific findings:

- Strengths such as self-regulation, perseverance, and love of learning predict academic success (Weber & Ruch, 2012b).

- Nurturing character strengths with strength-building activities and strength challenges within the school curriculum increases life satisfaction (Proctor et al., 2011).

- Character strengths such as kindness and teamwork predict fewer depression symptoms (Gillham et al., 2011).

- Assessing character strengths and nurturing them through interventions leads to greater student engagement in school (e.g., improved curiosity, love of learning, and creativity; Seligman et al., 2009).

- Check out many more findings in the research of this workbook.

Here is the bottom line: beyond raw IQ and the ability to absorb facts, applying one's character strengths is a fundamental 21st century skill for life success. Let's begin teaching our kids to look out for what is right in themselves, their environment, and others around them.

Who should use this book?

What's Right with This Picture? is for parents, teachers, and practitioners to work with kids to identify, nurture, and apply character strengths in their lives. This workbook is intended for kids ages 8-15 years old, but it can really be used with humanoids of any age!

How do you use this book?

The first step to becoming a character strength ninja is to expand your strength vocabulary. You can do this in the first section of this book (immediately after this introduction). After that, you'll dive into the next eight chapters devoted to a variety of fun stories. Read these stories with your kids and then try to answer the question: *What's Right with This Picture?* Focus on identifying character strengths exhibited by the main character of each story. After each story, there is a suggested "answer," which is simply one perspective on how the main character used his or her strengths in the story. Work with your kids to find other perspectives. Finally, after all the stories, you'll find the activity section of the book. Here you'll engage in games and other fun activities to apply your new and awesome knowledge of strengths!

Get in touch!

Although many people believe that the GoStrengths organization is made up of only animated characters, the truth is that we are real humanoids and would love to hear from you! Please send us an email at *go@gostrengths.com* or visit us at *gostrengths.com*.

Start by Expanding Your Strength Vocabulary!

If we were to list all the possible strengths in the world, this workbook would go on... well, forever. To make it easier, we're going to focus on the strengths found in something called the VIA classification which is supported by research and is limited to a list of 24 strengths we can all handle! You can read more about the VIA project in the reference section of this book.

Now, before we go on, let's take a minute to quickly define strengths. What are they? Your character strengths are part of your positive identity—they are what's best in you. Character strengths show up in the way you think, feel, and act. You are born with some strengths and can gain others over time through practice. But here's the thing, even though we all have strengths, most of us have a pretty limited strength vocabulary. It's not that we don't know what the words below mean; it's just that we may not use them as much as we could or should.

For example, it's more common for parents or teachers to say things such as, "Good job!" or "I'm proud of you!" or "Great going!" than "That was a very *creative* process you used!" or "Your *perseverance* when it comes to violin practice is really impressive!" or "You really showed *social intelligence* in that conversation with your friend!"

When we speak, we use the words and phrases that are most accessible to us or that pop into our minds first. As a youthling, you probably do the same thing. You may not think about your own character strengths or those in others because you simply don't use the strength vocabulary much. That's why the first step in this whole process of building up your character strengths is to ***expand*** your strength vocabulary!

On the next few pages, find the **24 character strengths** we've been talking about, along with short definitions. For the time being, just read the word, read the definition, and try to think about one time you or someone you know has used that strength. Ready? Go!

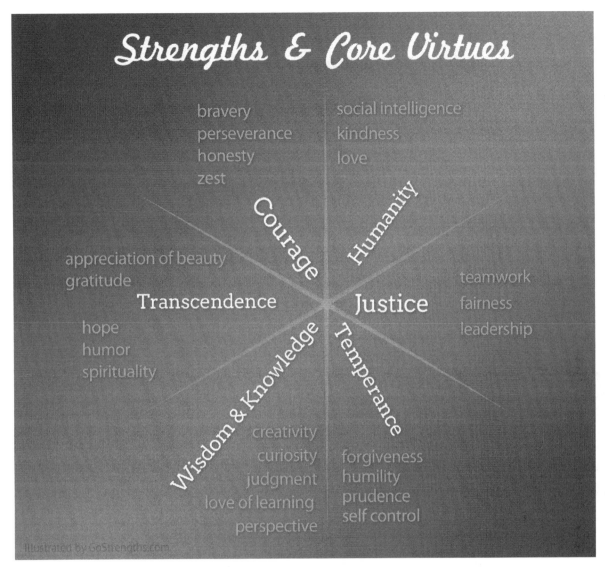

Appreciation of Beauty and Excellence: When you use this strength, you value beauty, excellence, and/or masterful skills in different areas of life. Related words: awe, wonder, elevation.

Bravery: When you use this strength, you take on threats, difficult times, or pain head on. You stand up for what you believe despite challenges. You act on your principles or what you believe in. Related words: courage, valor.

Capacity to Love and Be Loved: When you use this strength, you feel and show incredible affection for other people. You value close relationships, especially those relationships in which the other person/people feel the same way about you. You are open to receiving this same care and affection from others.

Creativity: When you use this strength, you think of new ways to do things and you have new ideas. Related words: originality, ingenuity

Curiosity: When you use this strength, you show interest in experiences for no other reason than the sake of having interest. You are fascinated with the world—you explore and discover. Related words: interest, novelty-seeking, openness to experience.

Fairness: When you use this strength, you treat people fairly and give everyone a chance. You don't let your personal feelings influence the way you judge people.

Forgiveness: When you use this strength, you do not stay angry with those who have done you wrong. You give people second chances. You don't hold grudges.

Gratitude: When you use this strength, you are aware of the good things that happen in your life. You are thankful for people and situations.

Honesty: When you use this strength, you act and speak truthfully. You are your genuine and sincere self. Related words: authenticity, integrity.

Hope: When you use this strength, you expect a good future and you work to achieve that future. Related words: optimism, future-mindedness, future-orientation.

Humility: When you use this strength, you allow your accomplishments to speak for themselves. You don't need to be in the spotlight. You are modest.

Humor: When you use this strength, you bring smiles to others' faces. You like to laugh and tease. You are playful and joke around. You see the lighter side of situations. Related trait: playfulness.

Judgment: When you use this strength, you think things through and look at things from all sides. You do not jump to conclusions. Related word: critical thinking.

Kindness: When you use this strength, you are generous to others. You help and do good deeds for others. Related words: generosity, nurturance, care, compassion, altruistic love.

Leadership: When you use this strength, you encourage a group to get things done and maintain good relationships. You make everyone in a group feel included. You are good at organizing activities and making them happen.

Love of Learning: When you use this strength, you like to master new skills and learn new things. You take any opportunity to learn whether inside a classroom or on your own.

Perseverance: When you use this strength, you work hard to finish what you've started. You're determined to reach your goals, no matter what your obstacles. You stay focused on your tasks. Related words: persistence, industriousness.

Perspective: When you use this strength, you have a point of view that makes sense to yourself and others. Your friends think you are wise and may turn to you for advice. Related word: wisdom.

Prudence: When you use this strength, you make choices carefully. You don't take on unnecessary risks. You don't say things that you might regret later.

Self-Regulation: When you use this strength, you stay in control over what you feel and what you do. You show discipline when it comes to things like appetite and emotions. Related word: self-control.

Social Intelligence: When you use this strength, you are aware of your own feelings as well as those of others. You know how to put others at ease. You know what to do to fit into various social situation. Related words: emotional intelligence, personal intelligence.

Spirituality: When you use this strength, you show strong beliefs about the higher purpose and meaning of the universe. You know where you fit within the larger scheme of things. Your beliefs influence your actions. Related words: faith, purpose.

Teamwork: When you use this strength, you work well as a member of a group or team. You are a dedicated, loyal teammate. You do your share of work in a group. Related words: citizenship, social responsibility, loyalty.

Zest: When you use this strength, you are excited and energized no matter what you're doing. You do things wholeheartedly. You live life like it's an adventure. Related words: vitality, enthusiasm, vigor, energy.

Story 1:

Sabrina Gets
Her Big Chance

Story 1: Sabrina Gets Her Big Chance

"Sabrina, come take a look at this!" Mrs. Durango called her daughter to the front hall. The mailman had just dropped off a chunk of letters, and Mrs. Durango was weeding out the junk mail.

"Coming, Mom!" Sabrina took the stairs two at a time and ran over. "What's up?"

"This flyer came in the mail. I think you should take a look. This sounds like it's right up your alley."

Sabrina took the bright purple flyer from her mother and read:

"Are you the next big Fliderdale Fashion Star? Do you have a passion for fashion? Enter the Fliderdale Fashion Design Contest and you could win a chance to put YOUR fashions on the runway. Come to the mall THIS Sunday at 2:00 p.m. and bring your best design! The winner will have real models wear their clothes! Be there or be square!"

Sabrina couldn't believe it. She read the flyer three times just to make sure she had all the details. This was her chance. She would finally be able to show everyone the clothes she had been working on for months!

"Well, Sabrina? Are you going to do it?" Mrs. Durango asked.

Sabrina thought for a moment. She had been so wrapped up in the excitement of the flyer that she hadn't stopped to consider her worries. *What if I don't win?* she thought. *Maybe the clothes I designed are not good enough. It might be embarrassing.* She sat down on the couch and stared at the flyer. *But even if I don't win, it will be a good experience,* she thought. *I'll get to see other designers' clothes and might be inspired. Also, I'll get to show off some of my own work. I have been working hard, and my designs are good. I might even win the prize!*

"I think I'll do it," Sabrina told her mom. "I think I have a good chance!"

"Wonderful," said Mrs. Durango. "You're going to be great!"

Suddenly, Sabrina realized that the contest was only four days away. "I have to get to work!" Sabrina jumped up and ran upstairs. She began to sketch and started looking through her fabric bin.

On Friday afternoon, Sabrina's best friend Nelly came over to model some of Sabrina's clothes. Sabrina had worked for hours the night before, making a blue sequin dress that zipped up the back. Zippers were hard, but Sabrina knew she was up for the challenge.

Nelly put on the dress, and as Sabrina tried to zip up the back, the zipper broke off and some of the fabric ripped.

"Oh no!" cried Nelly. "I ruined your project! I'm so sorry! What are you going to do now?" She turned around to stare at the gap where the two sides of the dress flapped open.

Sabrina looked thoughtfully at the zipper. "Don't worry, Nelly," Sabrina said. "I'll just do some more research to figure out a better zipper. It looks like this one wasn't secure. I know I can figure it out by Sunday if I put my mind to it."

"The dress is so beautiful," Nelly said as

she carefully took it off and changed into her regular clothes. "I hope you win, Sabrina! I'll be there cheering you on. What's the prize?"

Sabrina smiled. "They will put on a fashion show at the mall with real models wearing the winner's clothes. It's my dream! I can just picture it!"

On Sunday, Sabrina wrapped her dress in plastic and placed it carefully in her backpack. Her mother drove her to the mall, and Sabrina's brother Nik even came along for support, even though he claimed he was just going to check out the new skateboard shop that had just opened up.

When Sabrina and her family arrived, they saw a huge crowd gathered around the stage at the center of the mall. "Look at all these people!" Mrs. Durango said. "You go enter your name, Sabrina. We'll find a place where we can get a great view. Good luck!" Sabrina hugged her mom and walked to the contestants' table.

In front of her, a girl in hot pink leggings and a cool T-shirt was checking in. She was holding a beautiful polka dot dress. Sabrina's eyes widened.

"You made that?" Sabrina asked. "That is impressive."

"Thanks," said the girl. Sabrina checked herself in and then looked down at her own design. It wasn't as advanced as the polka dot dress. *Maybe the judges will see something unique in my dress and pick it anyway*, she thought.

"I can do this. I have a chance of winning," Sabrina whispered to herself as she took her dress backstage.

The crowd whooped and whistled as each contestant modeled his or her outfit for the judges. When Sabrina got on stage, she noticed her mom and Nik cheering loudly in the front. She felt thankful they were there to support her.

She twirled around, and the blue sequins sparkled in the bright stage lights. Then it was all over.

"Thank you all for participating in the first annual Fliderdale Fashion Design Contest!" The head judge's voice boomed over the microphone. The crowd grew silent.

"We had a lot of great contestants, and it was a very hard decision. But now it's time to announce the winner... Paige Miller! Let's give her a big round of applause!" The girl with the hot pink leggings, who had made the polka dot dress, smiled widely and hurried up to accept her prize ribbon.

Sabrina felt a little disappointed at first. She sighed and headed backstage to collect her things. But as Sabrina gave it some more thought, her mood began to lift. *I've been sewing for only a few months. I know that I'll get better at making clothes if I spend more time learning. I have already improved so much since I started!* Sabrina almost laughed remembering the first outfit she had ever tried to make--a skirt that ended up looking more like a mop. Her blue sequined dress was the best thing she had ever made.

I bet if I work hard, I can win this contest next year, or the year after! I know I'll be a famous designer someday.

And on the bright side, she thought as she ran to find her mom and brother, *I am feeling so inspired!*

What's Right With Sabrina?

One perspective: Sabrina shows great strength of character in this story. Specifically, she demonstrates a ton of hope. She is hopeful about her chances of winning the Fliderdale Fashion Design Contest and believes that if she tries hard, she can eventually succeed.

Sabrina also quickly bounces back from frustrations or setbacks. In this, she shows us her strength of perseverance. When her first attempt at making a zipper on her dress backfires, Sabrina doesn't quit. Instead, she does some research to figure out how to make the best zipper possible. Then she pushes forward in making her dress and does it with a great attitude.

Sabrina exhibits a lot of **bravery**—you have to be pretty brave to show off your creations in front of a huge crowd of people! Sabrina also shows **gratitude** when she takes a moment to appreciate that her mother and brother Nik are in the crowd, cheering her on and supporting her.

What do you think after reading the story? What's right with this picture?

_____

_____

_____

_____

Story 2:
Sam, the Ultimate Space Cadet

Story 2: Sam, the Ultimate Space Cadet

Sam could hardly sleep. He squeezed his eyes shut and tried to relax, but he was just too excited. Tomorrow, Sam and his classmates were taking a field trip to the space museum. They had been learning about planets and black holes in science class, and now they would spend the day exploring exhibits and maybe meeting real live astronauts.

Sam loved everything to do with space. In fact, he sometimes thought about being an astronaut when he grew up. He often built model space shuttles in his spare time and read books about intergalactic battles. Now, in just a few hours, he would be able to learn all about space from the pros. He felt alive and buzzing with energy—too much energy to sleep!

Somehow, Sam managed to doze off for a few hours, but he sprang awake when his alarm clock rang. He put on his NASA T-shirt and sprinted downstairs.

"Mom, what's for breakfast?" he half-shouted, knocking into his twin sisters, Lisa and Marisa.

"Wow, someone is in a good mood this morning," Lisa said, rubbing her tired eyes.

Marisa yawned. "Why are you so excited?"

"It's space museum day!" Sam started humming the theme song to *Star Wars* as he dug into a box of cereal. "I'm going to meet a real astronaut!"

Lisa and Marisa couldn't help but smile. Sam's enthusiasm was contagious—they found themselves singing the *Star Wars* theme song along with him.

At school, Sam was the first to get in line at the buses for the field trip. Sam's science teacher, whom everyone just called ScienceGuy, checked him off on his clipboard and handed him a stack of magazines.

"Hey, Sam," ScienceGuy said, "I know how much you love space, so I found these old space magazines in the teacher's lounge. Give them a read and let me know if you find anything interesting!"

"Whoa, thanks!" Sam said, stuffing the magazines in his backpack. "I will!" Sam could spend hours leafing through magazines with articles and pictures of space missions. Sometimes, he would read under the covers at night with a flashlight, long after everyone else had gone to sleep.

When Sam's good friend Daz showed up, the two of them talked about all of the things they couldn't wait to see. Daz was a member of the astronaut club, just like Sam.

"I hope they let us try out the antigravity machine!" Daz said, jumping up and down.

"I hope we get to try space food, like space ice cream!" Sam said. "I heard it's mostly this powder stuff that is freeze-dried... or something."

"Ugh, this is going to be so boring." Sam heard a voice behind him and turned. Trevor was slowly walking toward the buses. "Why do we have to go learn about nerdy space?"

Trevor had his arms folded across his chest and looked angry. He turned to ScienceGuy. "Why can't we go somewhere cool like the Monster Truck show? Space is for losers."

Sam felt his excitement drop a little bit. Maybe Trevor was right. Was it uncool to be so into space? His sisters sometimes made fun of him and called him "Space Geek." Maybe it was cooler to pretend that you weren't excited about anything. That's what Trevor and his friends did, and some people thought they were cool.

But then Sam shook his head. He shouldn't have to feel ashamed about being into space. *I have hobbies and interests*, Sam thought to himself. *I don't have to pretend to be bored all the time.* Suddenly Sam had an idea.

"Hey, Trevor," he said.

"Yeah? What?" Trevor replied, not that nicely.

"You know how you said you would rather go to a Monster Truck show than to the space museum?"

"Yeah, I want to see things crash and explode."

Sam smiled. "You know, Trevor, Monster Trucks aren't the only things that crash and explode. Did you know that meteorites, which are like giant space rocks, sometimes hit things at huge speeds and cause major crashes and explosions in outer space? It's like a giant Monster Truck show, but with no rules and no gravity!"

Trevor rubbed his sneaker on the concrete. "I guess that's kind of cool," he said. "I guess there are worse places than a space museum. Still kind of lame, though."

But as they boarded the bus, Sam noticed that Trevor was telling his group of friends about the meteorites. He had his hands up and was making big gestures, like two rocks exploding into pieces. ScienceGuy took Sam aside.

"Sam, I saw what you did there with Trevor," he said. "You really have a gift for spreading your enthusiasm to other people."

Sam beamed.

As the bus pulled away from the curb, Sam led his classmates in a round of the Fliderdale school song. "To infinity and beyond!" Sam shouted above the wind as the bus hit the highway. Then he started singing the *Star Wars* theme song, and everyone laughed and started singing along.

What's Right With Sam?

One perspective: Sam shows a lot of **zest** in this story. People with zest approach life with excitement and enthusiasm! They participate eagerly and seem to draw others in with their energy. Simply by being in the presence of a person with zest, others may begin to feel excited and amped up.

Sam has this effect on his sisters, who start to sing and laugh along with him in the morning. He also amps up Trevor, a student who seems determined to not enjoy the space museum. Sam's zest is clear when he gets his entire class excited for the field trip and leads them in song on the bus.

People with zest realize that it's not lame to show enthusiasm for life; in fact, it's the opposite of lame! When you have zest, you live life to the fullest and get more enjoyment out of your daily experience.

Sam also demonstrates **social intelligence**. He's good at relating to other people and understanding where they are coming from. He is even able to relate to Trevor and draw him into the field trip using something that Trevor is interested in—monster trucks.

Sam's interest in space also exhibits his **curiosity** and **love of learning**. He reads magazines and books about space to learn as much as he can, and we can guess that he will make the most of this field trip, listening carefully and asking lots of questions at the museum.

What do you think after reading the story? What's right with this picture?

Story 3:
Lisa's Skills
Put To The Test

Story 3: Lisa's Skills Put To The Test

"Quiet down, please!" Miss Crabtree called from her place on the podium. She tapped her conductor's baton on the music stand in front of her to get everyone's attention. The loud sounds of flutes and clarinets and horns and percussion gradually stopped.

"You have all been doing such a great job practicing for our spring concert," Miss Crabtree told her band students. "You sound wonderful."

One of the trumpet players played a few victory notes on his trumpet, and the band laughed. Even Miss Crabtree smiled.

"Since we have just a few weeks until our concert, it's time to discuss solo auditions." The room immediately began to buzz with the whispers of excited students. Miss Crabtree tapped her baton again to quiet the noise.

"Yes, solos are very exciting. For this concert, we'll have one clarinet solo and a drum solo. But I'd like to do something a little bit different. Instead of just having our first chair musicians play these solos, I would like to open solos up to the whole section. This means that any of the clarinet and percussion players can try out for a solo, whether you are first chair or sixth! Auditions will be this Monday after school. All right, class, have a great weekend!"

Lisa jumped up from her spot in the clarinet section and ran over to Miss Crabtree. "I want to sign up for an audition—for the clarinet solo!" she said excitedly.

Miss Crabtree smiled and shook her head. "There's no need to sign up, Lisa. Just come to the band room on Monday for try-outs. I am very happy to hear you are going to give this a try. I can't wait to hear you play."

Lisa grabbed her band folder and stuffed it in her backpack. She noticed that Marie, the girl who sat first chair, was doing the same.

"Hey, Marie, are you trying out for the solo?"

Marie nodded. "Are you?" Marie asked.

"Of course!" Lisa said. "Well, good luck anyway." *I'll have to practice all weekend to beat Marie*, Lisa thought to herself as she left school, swinging her clarinet by her side.

As soon as Lisa got home, she went to her room and pulled out her music. The solo was hard. There were many notes squeezed onto the page, and Lisa sometimes had a hard time reading music. She slowly worked out one note at a time and didn't stop working until her mother called her for dinner.

After dinner, Lisa went back to practicing. After an hour or so, she heard a knock on her bedroom door. "Come in!" she said, but she didn't put down her clarinet.

It was her twin sister, Marisa. "What are you doing?" Marisa asked.

"I'm practicing my clarinet solo for solo auditions in band," Lisa replied.

"Cool," said Marisa. "Nelly and I are going to see that new action movie—wanna come?"

Lisa frowned. She had been wanted to see *Space Storm 3* since she'd seen the previews on TV. It looked awesome, with lots of alien robot fights and explosions. She loved those kinds of movies.

"Well..." she said.

"Come on," Marisa said. "You probably need a break from that clarinet anyway."

But then Lisa thought about how much she wanted the solo. She wanted to play in front of everyone at the band concert and see her parents proudly beaming from the audience. She really wanted to be great at the clarinet.

"I think I'll pass," Lisa said. "I need to keep practicing."

"You sure?" Marisa asked, and then she was out the door.

The next day, after working on some math homework for Mr. Diddlydoo, Lisa got back to work. Her solo was starting to sound better—the notes flowed smoothly and clearly from her instrument, and she wasn't stumbling over the hard rhythm in measure 15. But it still wasn't perfect. She was concentrating so hard that she almost didn't notice her cell phone buzzing on her desk. She picked it up.

"Hello?" It was Alpana, one of Lisa's friends.

"Hey, it's me. Norma and Brittany and I are going to the mall to buy new dresses for the dance and check out cute guys. You have to come."

"Well..." Lisa did need a dress for the dance. She had been eyeing a light purple dress with tiny roses that she had seen at the mall last weekend with Marisa.

"Come on, Lisa! Don't be boring. We're all going!"

Lisa knew that if she went to the mall, her solo wouldn't be ready by Monday. After a long moment, she said, "I can't. I'm sorry, Alpana. I'll have to go to the mall with you guys another time."

After they hung up, Lisa felt a pang of unease. Maybe she was missing out on major bonding time with her friends. They'd probably have a blast and be talking at school about the cute dresses they tried on and the gorgeous guys at the food court. *I just have to focus on clarinet until Monday*, Lisa thought. *I can do this!*

On Monday, Lisa reached the band room feeling shaky. She looked down at her music, and all of the sudden the notes looked like a foreign language. She stopped for a moment and closed her eyes to calm herself down. *I've worked really hard, and I know this solo like the back of my hand. I have played it perfectly many times this weekend. Now it's time to show off my hard work.*

"Lisa?" Miss Crabtree said. "It's your turn."

As Lisa began to play, the music flowed easily from her clarinet. She was nervous, but her fingers seemed to know just what to do on their own. Eventually, Lisa stopped worrying about messing up and found herself enjoying the melody of the music. It was the first time she realized how much she loved playing the clarinet. When she finished, the rest of the students clapped.

"Lisa, that was excellent!" Miss Crabtree exclaimed. "I can tell you have worked really hard. Good job!"

After everyone had a turn, Miss Crabtree gathered her notepad and clipboard and stood up. "You have all worked hard, and I'm proud of each one of you. I would give you all solos if I could."

Lisa held her breath. "Let's start with the clarinet. Our spring concert clarinet solo will be performed by...

"... Lisa Silver."

Lisa jumped up from her chair with her fists in the air. "Yes!" she cried. She barely heard the rest of the announcements. All she could think about was wowing her family and friends with her music.

What's Right With Lisa?

One perspective: In this story, Lisa uses the **self-regulation** strength. She has a goal in mind, and she is able to delay gratification until she achieves that goal. Lisa is tested and tempted by multiple invitations. Her sister asks her to see a new movie she is interested in, and Alpana calls to invite her to a very tempting trip to the mall. However, Lisa uses a lot of self-regulation and gives up these more "fun" options in favor of practicing and working hard at her goal.

Lisa's ability to delay gratification pays off. Because she practices so diligently, Lisa impresses Miss Crabtree and is selected to perform a solo at the band spring concert. It is really hard to stay engaged in a solitary activity (practicing all alone) for hours and hours with no guarantee of success.

Lisa shows **bravery** in that she does not hesitate to approach Miss Crabtree about auditioning. Even though Lisa is not currently the first chair clarinet player, she is still brave enough to give the solo auditions a shot.

Lisa also exhibits **hope.** She believes that with effort she can achieve her goals. She does not get down on herself with pessimistic thinking and doesn't spend a lot of time thinking about the "What ifs"—such as "What if I fail?" or "What if I'm not good enough?" She assumes she has as good of a shot as anyone else.

What do you think after reading the story? What's right with this picture?

Story 4:
Rhonda Kicks It Into Action

Story 4: Rhonda Kicks It Into Action

"Each year, millions of sea animals are hurt due to littering the ocean water with trash. This picture shows a sea otter with its head stuck in the rings of a plastic soda can holder..."

Rhonda stared at her television in disbelief. She watched as a picture of a furry otter tangled in plastic popped up on the screen, while sad music played in the background. Animal shows were Rhonda's favorite. She loved watching documentaries about rare species of monkeys and programs about the world's most dangerous creatures. But this TV program wasn't pleasant at all. Instead, it talked all about how humans were damaging the world's animal life by failing to recycle. Rhonda couldn't believe that by just tossing a piece of plastic into the trash, rather than recycling, she might be harming poor little sea otters and other ocean life.

Someone has to do something about this! Rhonda thought. *I wonder what I can do. I'm not a part of the government or anything though....*

Rhonda was still thinking about the sea otters as she walked into school the next morning. She saw a group of girls drinking from plastic water bottles by the stairs. As the bell rang, signaling that first period was about to begin, she watched the girls toss their empty water bottles into the regular trash can one by one and head to class. Suddenly, Rhonda had an idea.

"This school needs recycling bins!" she said to herself aloud. She walked quickly to her classroom, her mind buzzing with enthusiasm. *How can we expect people to recycle with no recycling bins? Our school has to help protect the environment!*

At lunch, Rhonda rushed to the principal's office and approached the secretary, Ms. Daily.

"Ms. Daily, I need to speak with the principal as soon as possible!" she said, out of breath.

"He's in a meeting now, Rhonda," Ms. Daily said. "You'll have to wait a few minutes."

Rhonda took a seat in the principal's office and waited. She didn't mind waiting. All she could think about was achieving her goal. She waited and waited. Lunch passed, and the principal still hadn't emerged. Most kids would have given up by this point. But not Rhonda.

"Ms. Daily, I'll be back after school," Rhonda promised, and sure enough, when the final bell rang, Rhonda went straight back to the office. The principal's door was open this time.

Ms. Daily nodded at her. "Go ahead."

Rhonda took a deep breath and walked inside. The office was spacious and smelled like mahogany wood. The principal was seated at a large desk in the middle of the room, next to an American flag.

"Rhonda!" he said. "What can I do for you?"

"I would like to start a school-wide recycling program," Rhonda said confidently. She explained to the principal about the plastic and the sea otters. He nodded and folded his hands.

"Rhonda, I admire your enthusiasm for our planet," he said. Then he frowned. "But unfortunately, we just don't have the money for a recycling program. Since the budget has been cut, we can't afford to pay for all of the bins and, more importantly, the extra custodian hours needed to clear out those bins. The custodians have enough work to do already. I am truly sorry."

"But-but this is really important!" Rhonda cried. "What can be more important than the environment we live in?"

"I wish I could help," said the principal. "I wish I had the money to fund every great school program. Why don't you come back next year and see me? We may be able to start a program next year." He began to shuffle some papers, and Rhonda knew her meeting was over. She slowly got up from her chair and moved to the doorway.

"Thank you for your time," she said sadly. *Those poor baby sea otters...* "I'll be back next year," she said with determination.

Rhonda knew that to help the otters, she had to stick with her goal. Over the course of that school year, she brainstormed ways to convince the principal of the importance of recycling. She spent months working on large posters explaining how plastics might easily be reused to make new materials.

At the start of the next school year, Rhonda positioned herself at the front doors of the school building with a stack of flyers in hand.

"COME JOIN THE FIRST EVER FLIDERDALE EARTH CLUB!" the flyers read in bright green ink. Over the summer, Rhonda had decided that she would try to start an Earth Club to raise support for her recycling program. The club might have to work for years and years to accomplish all of Rhonda's goals! Her classmates began to grab her flyers and read.

"Saving our environment is important! Come one, come all, help us make Fliderdale a greener place!" Rhonda called out as students walked by.

"This sounds awesome, Rhonda," said Nelly, one of Rhonda's classmates. "What kinds of projects will the Earth Club do?"

"My first goal is to raise money for recycling bins in every classroom! Then the Earth Club members can empty out the bins so the custodians don't have to!" Rhonda said.

"Sounds cool!" said Nelly. "Where do I sign up?" As Nelly reached for Rhonda's sign-up sheet, Daz pushed his way through the crowd of kids that had formed.

Daz was always picking on Rhonda, and today was no exception. "That doesn't sound fun; that sounds lame. Who cares about the environment anyway?"

Rhonda frowned. "You should care, Daz," she said, but she didn't get angry or down on her project. "If we don't take care of the environment, we will be in big trouble in the future. You don't have to join, anyway," she said, and Daz sulked away.

On the second week of school, Rhonda made an appointment to see the principal. She came in and brought her posters with her.

"Well, it's a new school year," she said to the principal, smiling. "I said I'd be back, and here I am."

"I knew you wouldn't give up on a cause you believed in," the principal said. "Let's hear some of those ideas."

Over the next few months, Rhonda and her small group of Earth Club members raised money selling baked goods on the lawn during lunch period. They spent hours and hours baking cookies and brownies and cupcakes. When Rhonda finally was able to purchase blue recycling buckets, she noticed with dismay that not everyone was using the buckets. Kids were throwing their plastic bottles and bags right into the trash, ignoring the blue buckets!

"Why is this happening?" Rhonda wailed at one of their Earth Club meetings a few weeks later.

"Maybe we should just give up, Rhonda. People don't seem to care about the Earth," Nelly said feeling a little hopeless.

Rhonda thought for a moment. She had already spent a lot of time going from classroom to classroom, educating people on how and when to use the buckets. She had spoken with teachers about encouraging their classes to recycle. But kids still weren't cooperating. What else could she do?

"Let's not give up yet," she told her fellow Earth Club members. "I have one more idea."

Rhonda decided that what students needed were incentives, or rewards for recycling. She set up a school-wide contest--the classroom with the most recycled items in its blue buckets at the end of each week would win a point. At the end of the month, the class with the most points would win a pizza party!

Suddenly, Rhonda's blue buckets began to fill up. Everyone wanted to win the prize! The Earth Club was now busy carrying giant piles of bottles to the recycling plant.

"See, Nelly? I told you we could do it!" Rhonda said happily as they carried the last of the recycled materials to her mom's car. She pictured the sea otters swimming happily in a clean and clear blue ocean. But there was still so much to do. Rhonda had made a list of Fliderdale environmental projects, and she wasn't about to stop after reaching just one goal. One down, tons more to go!

What's Right With Rhonda?

One perspective: In this story, Rhonda uses the strength **perseverance.** She pursues her goals despite obstacles that get in her way—she keeps going and absolutely refuses to give up. Even when she experiences rejection with the principal, she picks herself up and brainstorms new ways to succeed.

Rhonda shows **creativity** when it comes to solving problems. She found a creative way to save the school money by creating the Earth Club and recruiting members to empty the recycling bins and take them to the recycling plant themselves. She also really motivated students to recycle by creating a pizza party reward for the classroom that did the best job at filling up its bin.

Rhonda demonstrates great **leadership** by creating a club, motivating members to strive toward a common goal, and organizing and executing plans to make it all happen.

Rhonda also shows **appreciation of beauty and excellence**. She respects and savors the beauty in nature and animals.

What do you think after reading the story? What's right with this picture?

_____

_____

_____

Story 5:
Tomas's Simple Exercise

Story 5: Tomas's Simple Exercise

Tomas was not happy. He sat in his room alone, trying to focus on the book in front of him. But he couldn't make himself read the pages. He was too upset.

Why am I so lame? Tomas thought to himself. He heard his older sister Alpana run downstairs and slam the door behind her. Their mom, Mrs. Krishnamurti, called out, "Don't be home too late!" Alpana was always going fun places with groups of giggling girlfriends. She always seemed so relaxed; her life was so easy.

Why can't I be like that? Tomas thought. He tossed his book off the bed and lay face down on his favorite blue pillow.

Tomas had been invited to Sam's house that night for a small hang-out. Just a couple of guys from their class, some videogames, and lots of snacks. Tomas had been really excited at first... before he remembered Sam's dog, Smoocher. Tomas was terrified of dogs. He hated the way they would jump all over him and bark loudly. It would be way too scary to go over to Sam's house and risk seeing Smoocher. He hadn't wanted to tell Sam the truth. Instead, he told Sam that he was too busy to come over.

Now, Tomas sat alone on a Friday night, with nowhere to go. He felt mad at himself. "I have a terrible life," Tomas said out loud to nobody.

Suddenly, Tomas heard a knock on the door. His mother peeked her head in. "Tomas? What are you doing?"

"Nothing," Tomas said.

"You look upset. Is something wrong?"

"No. Well, yeah. Everything is wrong. Nothing is good." Tomas folded his arms across his chest.

"Nothing is good?" his mother repeated. "Nothing at all?"

"I can't think of one single thing that is good in my life," said Tomas.

His mother sighed. She disappeared from the doorway, and Tomas thought that she was gone for good. But a few moments later she reappeared with a small red book.

"Tomas, I have an assignment for you," she said, handing the book to him. He flipped through it.

"It's just a bunch of blank pages," he said, confused.

"Yes. Every morning when I wake up, I write down five things that I am thankful for. I keep my own journal, just like this one. Sometimes I write down small things, like the sunshine or fresh fruit. Sometimes they are larger things, like seeing my children smile." Mrs. Krishnamurti tapped on the red book. "Now it's your turn."

"I don't know..." said Tomas. "How is this going to make things better?"

Tomas's mom smiled. "Give it a chance, Tomas," she said, before heading off to bed.

The next day, Tomas dragged himself out of bed and reluctantly grabbed the red book his mom had given him. He tucked it into the back pocket of his jeans and went downstairs. In the cabinet, he saw his favorite flavor of Pop-Tarts: strawberry. "All right!" Tomas said, and eagerly opened the box. *Thank you, Mom*, he thought.

Then he paused. I should put this in my journal. He opened the journal to a fresh page and wrote in the date. Then he wrote WHAT I AM THANKFUL FOR in big letters. Underneath, he filled in "Strawberry Pop-Tarts" and "Mom." *This is easy*, Tomas thought. He was so busy filling out his notebook that he barely noticed the phone ring.

"Tomas! Telephone!" his mother called from upstairs. Tomas picked up. "Hello?"

"Hey, it's Sam!"

"Oh, uh, hey, Sam," Tomas said. He felt guilty for skipping out on Sam's party. "What's up? How was your party?"

"It was pretty fun. I'm sorry you couldn't make it yesterday. It would have been more fun with you there--you're the best at Zombie Apocalypse 3!"

Tomas smiled. He was pretty good at that video game. He had spent years and years perfecting his technique and was finally able to reach the highest level of the game. And Sam hadn't forgotten about him.

"Anyway, do you want to go shoot some hoops later at the park?" Sam asked.

"Yeah, sure!" Tomas said eagerly. "I'll meet you there soon!"

When the boys hung up, Tomas felt happy. He pulled out his journal and wrote down "Friendship with Sam" and "Zombie Apocalypse 3." His list of things to be thankful for was quickly filling up!

Wow, Tomas thought, as he ran upstairs to change into his basketball shorts. I actually have a lot to be thankful for. And the day has only just started!

What's Right With Tomas?

One perspective: In this story, Tomas shows a ton of **gratitude**. With the help of his mom, Mrs. Krishnamurti, Tomas learns the importance of being thankful and appreciating things in his everyday life.

Tomas is also being **open-minded**. He actually tries his mom's suggestion to keep a gratitude journal. He doesn't just immediately dismiss her journal idea as stupid. Even though he is skeptical, Tomas gives the exercise a try.

Using his journal, Tomas is able to pull himself out of a sad mood by keeping an out for things to be thankful for. His gratitude makes him feel good and opens his eyes to the fact that life isn't so terrible after all—in fact, his life is pretty good! He uses the strength of **perspective**, or looking at his life in a different way, to feel better.

What do you think after reading the story? What's right with this picture?

_____

_____

_____

_____

_____

_____

_____

_____

_____

_____

_____

_____

_____

_____

_____

_____

Bonus: Check out this cool animation on keeping a gratitude journal:

http://bit.ly/gratjournal

Story 6:

Yoon-hee's Great Adventure

Story 6: Yoon-hee's Great Adventure

Yoon-hee was walking slowly home from school, holding a book in her hands. She had been reading this book about rainforests, and she was so absorbed in the pages that she barely noticed anything around her. It was just so cool! Rainforests were home to thousands of unknown creatures and insects, and had tons of leafy layers.

Yoon-hee hoped to visit a rainforest at some point in the future. She imagined herself hiking through the thick trees, waving to three-toed sloths and stepping over brightly colored bugs.

When she finally put her book down, she looked up and noticed that a new bookstore had opened up right by her house. Yoon-hee loved exploring new places. She was usually very shy and often had a hard time talking to people, but she liked to enter new worlds, to imagine that she was in another land or on a new planet. She liked to observe and understand her surroundings.

Bells jingled as Yoon-hee entered the store called Bookworm, which had rows and rows of books. Old books, new books, books with shiny covers. Yoon-hee loved the smell of books.

"Hello!" One of the workers with gray hair and large eyes smiled as Yoon-hee walked past the first row of fiction novels. "Welcome to Bookworm. Feel free to look around!"

Yoon-hee could barely contain her excitement. She flipped through various books of poetry, her favorite. She read poetry lines and copied them in the poetry notebook that she always carried for inspiration. She read the inside flaps of the new nonfiction books and finally bought a book about whales.

There is so much out there to learn, Yoon-hee thought to herself. *Even by the time I'm an adult, I'll know only one tiny piece of all there is to know about the world! I had better learn as much as I can each day.*

Yoon-hee continued to explore the store. She tried a fudge sample from the cafe, a food she had never tried before. It tasted like heaven, chocolate and peanut butter swirled together.

Yoon-hee was just about to head home when she noticed a bunch of flyers sitting on a windowsill on the way out. She grabbed one. It was for a poetry class—once a week held right in the bookstore. "Come share your poetry with other writers!" the flyer read. The first class was that night, in just twenty minutes.

Yoon-hee felt conflicted. She loved poetry and wanted to be inspired by other writers. But she had never shared her poems before. They were very personal poems about her world, and she wasn't sure if she would ever be able to share them with anyone else. What if people made fun of her and thought her poems were bad?

At the same time, Yoon-hee wondered whether people's comments and feedback might help her improve her writing. She wanted to be a better poet. She wanted to learn from people who had lots of experience and pick up as many writing tips as possible.

Yoon-hee decided to call her mom and see if she could stay at Bookworm and attend the first poetry class. She got the go-ahead from her mom!

Yoon-hee didn't bring any of her work with her, but she sat and listened carefully to other poets. She took notes when something excited her and even thought of an idea for a brand new poem during the class.

Afterward, Yoon-hee gathered up her things. She wanted to approach a man named Owen whose poetry had really spoken to her, but she felt nervous. *What if he doesn't want to talk to me?* she thought. *I am not good at making conversation. It might be awkward.*

Suddenly, she felt a tap on her shoulder. It was Owen.

"I haven't seen you before," he said with a smile.

"I'm Yoon-hee," she said quietly. "I'm new. I loved your poem about San Francisco."

"Thanks," said Owen. "That poem is very special to me. I started writing it while on a trip to Australia, actually..."

Owen began telling Yoon-hee stories, and she found that he was actually really easy to talk to! She started to ask him questions. How did he get started writing? Could he recommend any great poetry books for her? What should she do when she started to get writer's block and couldn't write?

Yoon-hee returned home to her neighborhood filled with a ton of new information. She had learned so much in just one day--about rainforests, art, food, and poetry. She vowed to come back to the poetry class next time with a brand new story, and to absorb as much poetry as she possibly could.

What's Right With Yoon-hee?

One perspective: Yoon-hee shows a ton of **curiosity**! She is interested in learning as much as possible about the world. She reads lots of books on a variety of subjects, from rainforests, to whales, to poetry. She explores a new bookstore, taking her time to experience all that it has to offer. Yoon-hee is curious about food, art, and writing.

Yoon-hee displays **bravery** by taking a risk and exploring a new setting, a poetry workshop.

Yoon-hee also shows her **love of learning** in the story. She enjoys soaking up new experiences and gets really into the books that she reads. Yoon-hee is able to lose herself in books she is reading or poems she is writing, immersing herself to the point that the rest of the world fades away.

What do you think after reading the story? What's right with this picture?

_____

_____

_____

_____

_____

Story 7:
Tomas's Big Crush

Story 7: Tomas's Big Crush

Sabrina and her friend Nelly walked past Tomas and Sam on their way to lunch. Tomas felt like he was floating on air. It was almost as though his heart had expanded to twelve times its normal size. He took a deep breath to steady himself and turned to his friend Sam.

"Do you think Sabrina even knows I'm alive?" he asked Sam hopefully.

Tomas had been in love with Sabrina for a long time. At least, he thought he loved her. Every time he was around her, he felt a burst of happiness. He felt that he wanted to know everything about her and tell her all of his secrets. She was so friendly and nice to everyone, and when she talked to Tomas, it seemed like she really cared. She also had lots of passions, like fashion design, which Tomas admired.

Tomas didn't know if Sabrina would ever like him back, but just being near her was enough to fill him with joy. When Tomas was in a bad mood, he would sometimes think of Sabrina laughing at one of his jokes, in his imagination, and he would feel better.

"Of course Sabrina knows who you are," Sam said. Sam was a good friend. He was always trying to boost Tomas's confidence. "You've sat in front of her in math class for the past two years."

"Yeah, but we didn't really talk much," Tomas admitted. Every time he tried to work up the courage to ask Sabrina a question, he would chicken out. One time, he dropped his pencil, and she picked it up and smiled. Another time, she asked him if he was going to the Fliderdale Fall Festival, and all he managed to say was, "Yes."

"You should try talking to her, Tomas," Sam said. "You have a great sense of humor and you are smart. Just strike up a conversation."

"I guess you're right." Tomas smiled at his best friend. In that moment, he wanted to hug Sam and tell him how much he appreciated his support. It made him feel good to know that Sam cared about him. He gave him a high five instead of a hug before he and Sam joined the lunch line.

That afternoon, Tomas was waiting for his mom to pick him up from school when he noticed Sabrina sitting alone on a bench outside of the front entrance. She was listening to music and staring into space.

Tomas's stomach jumped into his throat. This was his chance! Sabrina wasn't surrounded by girlfriends, so it would be less intimidating to approach her. But what should he say? Maybe he should just ask her what song she was listening to. He wiped some sweat from his brow and slowly walked over to the bench.

"Hey Sabrina," Tomas said quietly. He already felt those feelings coming back—the butterflies in his stomach, the urge to break out into a huge smile.

"Hey Tomas," Sabrina said. She took one of her earbuds out and grinned. "What's up?"

"Oh, nothing much, I'm just waiting for my ride. What are you listening to?" So far so good. She was at least talking to him.

"It's a band called Lion's Den? Have you heard of it?" Sabrina squinted up at him.

Tomas's heart flipped. "Lion's Den? I love Lion's Den!" Tomas had all of their albums, even the ones from before they were famous. He couldn't believe that Sabrina liked one of his favorite bands. She was even cooler than he had thought! Tomas was glowing on the inside as he and Sabrina talked and bonded over their favorite songs from the band's newest album. They formed a connection.

"Yeah, and I'm going to see them play next weekend at the mall," Tomas said excitedly. "I can't wait to hear them live!"

"No way!" Sabrina's eyes widened. "That is so awesome!"

Suddenly, Tomas had an idea. "Hey, do you by any chance... want to go with me to the concert?" As soon as the words came out of his mouth, Tomas felt himself regret it. What if she said no? The three-second pause waiting for her response felt like forever.

"Sure! I would love to!" Sabrina said. Then she spotted her mom's van pulling into the parking lot. "I have to go, but we'll talk before then. I can't wait!" She reached over and impulsively gave Tomas a big hug before running to the car.

Tomas sat down on the bench. He had never felt so happy and alive in his entire life. Maybe he and Sabrina would get to know each other better, and maybe even date, and become boyfriend and girlfriend. They would watch movies together and hold hands in the hallways at school.

But he was getting ahead of himself. For now, he would go home and replay their conversation over and over. He would think about how much fun the Lion's Den concert would be. Tomas smiled from ear to ear.

What's Right With Tomas?

One perspective: Tomas is a person who has the **capacity to love and be loved**. Tomas recognizes that he has a lot of love to share and seeks out lasting relationships with friends and with girls he admires.

Tomas feels a variety of loving feelings throughout the story. He is in love with Sabrina and hopes to get close to her through the Lion's Den concert. But he also experiences a different kind of love, the love between two best friends who have each other's backs and who encourage and support one another. The strength of love is not just about crushes and romance, though that can be an exciting part of love. Love is also about our ability to care for other people, and how open we are to receiving care in return. Tomas hopes that his love for Sabrina will grow into a friendship or a relationship in which they can care about one another.

Tomas is super **brave** to ask Sabrina out on a date to the concert even though he is really nervous. If you've ever worked up the nerve to talk to a crush, you know how scary it can be!

Tomas also demonstrates **zest** for the Lion's Den band and his excitement for musical experiences.

What do you think after reading the story? What's right with this picture?

Story 8:
Marisa vs. Lisa: Sister vs. Sister

Story 8: Marisa vs. Lisa: Sister vs. Sister

Marisa wiped the sweat off her brow and jogged over to join the rest of her teammates in a group huddle. Their team captain, Allison, was speaking in a loud whisper, calling out different plays and trying to motivate her crew.

The Fliderdale Hyenas were down 3-0 at the first soccer game of the season, and it was already halftime. They seriously needed to catch up.

Marisa wasn't the best soccer player, but she was a dependable member of the team. She always tried to make herself open, played defense with tons of enthusiasm, and cheered for her teammates from the benches.

Marisa loved that feeling of belonging to something bigger than herself. She loved being just one part of a whole, a team of strong and athletic girls. Out on the field, she had her teammates' backs no matter what. She just wished she could be more supportive of her soccer girls off the field.

Marisa's twin sister Lisa loved making fun of the Fliderdale girls' soccer team. Lisa had decided that a lot of Marisa's teammates were lame because they were more into sports than things like makeup and fashion. She would say things such as, "How are the Fliderdale Fashion Nightmares?" when Marisa came home from practice and would make faces when she saw Marisa's teammates wearing baggy T-shirts and shorts.

Marisa thought Lisa was probably jealous. When Marisa had long practices after school, Lisa had to take the bus home alone. Also, Lisa wasn't good at any organized sports—unless you counted speed shopping. But Marisa couldn't help but feel hurt when Lisa and her friends joked about how uncool the Hyenas were.

Normally, Marisa would just roll her eyes and pretend it didn't bother her. But she never defended her teammates or told Lisa to stop insulting them. Marisa felt guilty for not standing up for her soccer friends and for caring about what other people thought.

She felt especially guilty when Allison asked her to sit with the team at lunch and she made up some lame excuse because she didn't want Lisa and her girlfriends to see her eating with "uncool" kids.

The soccer team spilled back out onto the field to face their rivals, the Wildcats, once more. The ground was muddy from a recent rainfall. Everyone was slipping and sliding, and Marisa laughed as a shower of mud hit her legs.

She got ahold of the ball and passed to Allison. Allison managed to maneuver the ball past a pack of Wildcats and scored! Yes!

Marisa ran up and pulled Allison into a giant hug. Their teammates surrounded them, jumping up and down. It was the best feeling in the world. She loved these girls.

After the game, Marisa headed toward the locker rooms with Chelsea and Lee, two girls on the team. They had lost, 4-2, but they were still proud of their comeback. The team was planning to go out for ice cream to celebrate. As they were making their way through the grass, still muddy and sweaty and laughing about the game, Lisa and two friends rushed over to Marisa.

"Hey, don't take too long in the locker room," Lisa said. "We're going to grab burgers."

Marisa froze. Her soccer friends stood on either side of her.

"Um, I might have other plans," Marisa said hesitantly.

Lisa crossed her arms over her chest. "What do you mean?"

"I think... I'm going out for ice cream with the team."

"So you're ditching us for these girls?" Lisa said. The way she said "these girls" made it clear that she did not think they were cool. At all.

Marisa began to feel uncomfortable. She looked at Chelsea and Lee, who kept silent but looked upset. Marisa took a deep breath.

"Lisa, these are my friends. And they're really awesome people. Did you see Chelsea's defense out there? And Lee's goal-keeping? We just played a great game, and we're going out for ice cream. You're welcome to join us."

Lisa looked surprised. She shrugged her shoulders. "Whatever," she said. "We're getting burgers. Just text me later." Then she and her friends walked off.

Marisa shook her head. Her sister would always be a little bit difficult, but maybe someday she would understand that "coolness" wasn't about clothes and bags and shoes. She put one arm around each teammate.

"Let's go, Hyenas!" she called out, as loudly as she could.

What's Right With Marisa?

One perspective: Marisa uses her strengths of **teamwork** and **citizenship** in this story. Someone who has a strong sense of citizenship isn't simply a member of a group or team. Rather, he or she works well with fellow group members, offering support and standing up for group members when others are putting them down.

Although Marisa is hesitant at first to stand up to her sister and her sister's friends, she eventually realizes that she must support her soccer teammates. She is loyal to them and follows through with her plans to get ice cream after the game, rather than ditching them for a "cooler" plan. She learns to be there for her teammates both on and off the field. This makes her a good citizen or team member that her soccer friends can respect and count on.

Marisa also shows **zest** in her enthusiasm for soccer. She has found an activity that she genuinely enjoys, and she feels passionate and energetic on the soccer field. She is brave to go against what is considered "cool" and "uncool," and to decide for herself who she wants to be friends with.

What do you think after reading the story? What's right with this picture?

_____

_____

_____

_____

_____

_____

_____

_____

_____

_____

_____

_____

_____

_____

_____

_____

_____

_____

Activities

What's Right with This Picture?

Can you name all the things right with this picture? What kinds of strengths do you see being demonstrated?

Strengths Word Search

Can you find all of the strengths hidden in this word search? Look horizontally, vertically, diagonally, backward, and forward to find them all!

```
O P T I M I S M J U D G M E N T E V O L
W I S D O M O Y T I R G E T N I T E M W
R R R Y X P C S S E N R I A F C H S J Y
A P P R E C I A T I O N O F B E A U T Y
Y G N I R A E L F O E V O L I F I N C
T P Y E L T L E S P Z K L M S X L G I S
I E T Y D Y I Q C E E L I U E A O T Y O
C R I F T U N A S N X R H N U R I Y P E
I S V P S T T L G A T S T D Z C E S C
T I I I E E I B O N R I P E N N Y U N
N S T L R A L B T E R R E N E M E R H E
E T A E E M L R K A I T S V I C I S S D
H E E A T W I A E P R H N N E O T O S U
T N R D N O G V S P I G D O S S P I X R
U C C E I R E E T P O E C I C R R J V P
A E H R D K N R W N D H T A U F R E Z E
D T U S E U C Y A N H Y E P E Z L H P M
G Y M H S S E N E V I G R O F G R E Y L
I U O I P S A S G E N E R O S I T Y S L
Z U R P J N S O R I G I N A L I T Y S E
```

Word Bank:

Creativity

Originality

Curiosity

Interest

Open-mindedness

Judgment

Love of Learning

Perspective

Wisdom

Bravery

Persistence

Perseverance

Integrity

Authenticity

Zest

Enthusiasm

Love

Kindness

Generosity

Social Intelligence

Citizenship

Teamwork

Fairness

Leadership

Forgiveness

Mercy

Prudence

Self-control

Appreciation of Beauty

Gratitude

Hope

Optimism

Humor

Spirituality

Purpose

Strengths Crossword Puzzle

Use the clues below to fill in the crossword with strengths! The answers could be one of the 24 strengths you've learned about or a related word.

Across:

4. Controlling what you feel and do; being disciplined; controlling your appetites and emotions.

5. Performing good deeds for others.

7. Taking on danger, challenges, difficulty, or pain; acting on your beliefs even if they're not popular.

10. Taking an interest in experiences; exploring and discovering new things.

11. Expecting the best in the future and working to achieve it.

12. Liking to laugh and tease; bringing smiles to other people; seeing the lighter side of things.

13. Valuing something awe-inspiring, beautiful, excellent.

16. Encouraging a group to get things done while maintaining good relationships with everyone in the group.

17. Working well as a member of a group or team; showing that you are a responsible member of a community.

18. Being yourself; taking responsibility for your feelings and actions.

19. Letting your accomplishments speak for themselves.

20. Having fun in mastering new skills.

22. Being thankful for good things that happen; taking time to express thanks.

23. Having ways of looking at the world that make sense to yourself and others.

24. Finishing what you start; not giving up when faced with obstacles.

Down:

1. A feeling of strong affection for someone or something.

2. Giving people a second chance; not being vengeful.

3. Being careful about your choices; not taking unnecessary risks; not saying or doing things that you might later regret.

6. Having clear beliefs about a higher purpose, the meaning of life, the meaning of the universe.

8. Finding new ways to do or think about things.

9. Being aware of the motives and feelings of other people and yourself.

14. Being willing to consider different ideas or opinions.

15. Approaching life with excitement and energy; feeling alive and activated.

21. Treating all people the same.

My Greatest Strengths

Everyone has super awesome powers! What is awesome about you? What are your greatest strengths that you use at school, home, or other places? Think about your 5 greatest strengths and write them in the space in the middle of the image below.

Bonus! With the help of your teacher or parent, you can also take a short survey that helps you identify your greatest strengths. Find the survey here: *http://bit.ly/viayouthsurvey*

Strength Story

One of the best ways to get to know your strengths is to write a story about how you've used one of them! You can see an example of strength stories by watching this animation: *http://bit.ly/strengthstories*

Now, try to write your own in the space below or on a separate piece of paper!

Strength Drawing

You've done a lot of writing, but now you're going to switch gears and do some drawing! What do you look like when you're using one of your strengths? We asked Yoon-hee to draw her using one of her great strengths and this is what she came up with:

Yoon-hee says, "This is me being **creative** with a science project. I created the universe in a shoe box! I'm smiling because I'm **grateful** my mom helped me out with some ideas on how I could make all the little pieces inside the shoebox stick together.

Now, think of when you recently used one of your greatest strengths. Draw a picture of what that looks like in the space below.

Strength Spotting

People use strengths every day before our very eyes, but lots of times we don't notice it's happening. That is, until now. Now that you're familiar with strengths, you're qualified to be a strengths spy!

Here is your first mission: Spot each of the strengths below at least once in real life situations. As soon as you spot a strength, write about it below. Keep going until you spot all 24 strengths!

Strength Spotted	What did you spot?	Why was it awesome?	The Date
Example: Forgiveness	*I saw my sister forgive our little brother for messing up her room.*	*She was really, really mad. She could have told on him, but she decided to forgive him instead. That was pretty awesome.*	*December 25th*
Appreciation of Beauty and Excellence			
Bravery			
Capacity to Love and Be Loved			
Creativity			

Curiosity			
Fairness			
Forgiveness			
Gratitude			
Honesty			
Hope			
Humility			
Humor			
Judgment			
Kindness			
Leadership			

Love of Learning			
Perseverance			
Perspective			
Prudence			
Self-Regulation			
Social Intelligence			
Spirituality			
Teamwork			
Zest			

Strength Missions

Practice your strengths by doing these 99 strength missions! Try doing a different mission each day to develop some new strengths.

Mission 1: Appreciation of Beauty - Do you have a favorite food? Eating something you truly love is an awesome experience! Today, grab one of your favorite foods and eat it very, very slowly. Smell the food before you eat it, chew slowly and delight in the flavors, savor every bite, and really submerge yourself in the experience. Write down at least three reasons that your culinary delight was a beautiful experience.

Mission 2: Creativity - Get a few magazines and flip through the pages. Tear out every word and photo that pops out at you. Don't stop to think about it; just rip away every time you feel yourself pause over a word or photo. On a poster or piece of cardboard, make a collage of the words and photos. Hang the "me" poster in your house somewhere.

Mission 3: Capacity to Love and Be Loved - Leave someone you love a trail of clues leading them from place to place. Try to make each place one that has meaning for both of you. Have the last clue lead them to you and tell them how much they mean to you.

Mission 4: Love of Learning - Leonardo da Vinci wrote most of his notes backward so they could not be read unless someone held them up to a mirror. Today, learn to write backward and/or upside down. You will learn something new and also will use a creative part of your brain. If you're having a hard time figuring out what to write, try your name!

Mission 5: Gratitude - Cut out or take a picture of something you take for granted. Ice? Water? Toilet paper? Sheets? Maybe it's something you NEVER think about, like the trees that give us air. Today, make it a visual reminder of what you are grateful for.

Mission 6: Capacity to Love and Be Loved - Draw up a list of things to do that would make up the perfect day with someone important to you. Include every detail—what you would do, where you would eat, how you would get there. Type it up or write it neatly and present it to them.

Mission 7: Honesty - For one entire day, do not lie. In big and small things, speak only the truth!

Mission 8: Humor - Find a picture in a newspaper or magazine and make up a humorous caption for it that has nothing to do with the actual picture.

Mission 9: Social Intelligence - Follow the Golden Rule today = *Do unto others as you* *would have them do unto you*. What does that rule mean to you? This task requires you to constantly remember how you are treating every person that you meet. At the end of the day, write about your experience.

Mission 10: Kindness - Watch out for acts of kindness today! Find other people who are being generous, pleasant, kind, and giving. Write these acts down in a list. How many did you find?

Mission 11: Hope - Make a plan to do something you've always wanted to do—a dream. Write it out!

Mission 12: Spirituality - Find a minute to be alone. Breathe in and out for at least two minutes. Try not to think of anything; concentrate on breathing. Write about your experience afterward.

Mission 13: Perspective - Today, do everything with the opposite hand that you normally use. Try your best to stick with it! How did it feel?

Mission 14: Fairness - Find a book or movie about someone who fights for justice and fairness. What do you admire most about this person? What motivated this person?

Mission 15: Prudence - Save energy today by not keeping the refrigerator open too long, by shutting off lights, and by not watching TV!

Mission 16: Kindness - Tuck a kind note under at least three different places today as a pleasant surprise for someone down the road.

Mission 17: Curiosity - Fingerprint yourself. You can do this using talcum powder or even a piece of tape. Use the Internet to find out what your fingerprint type says about your personality.

Mission 18: Spirituality - Take in a deep breath while counting in your mind to four. Hold the breath in while counting to eight. Exhale the breath while counting to twelve. Repeat this at least five times. How do you feel?

Mission 19: Social Intelligence - Find out two things about a friend that you didn't know before by asking them about themselves. Be thoughtful about the questions you ask them.

Mission 20: Gratitude - Give someone a handwritten note of thanks for something they've done recently for you. Make sure you include the specific reason you're thankful for what they've done.

Mission 21: Love of Learning - Take a few minutes to read about something you're really interested in and find out at least one fact you didn't know before.

Mission 22: Fairness - Think of a time when you judged someone and later found out that your view was wrong. Write down what you could do differently to avoid doing the same thing in the future.

Mission 23: Humor - Exaggerate with silly emotions today. After you're done brushing your teeth, shout for joy, "Yes! I did it!" When you get to school, scream out "Woooohooo—yes, another day of school!" See if you can make yourself or someone else laugh.

Mission 24: Hope - Draw a line on a piece of paper. This line represents your life. Write on it the years and mark off accomplishments, landmarks, things you're proud of... make it as long as you would hope to live, and include on it any future events you would like to see in this lifetime. Children? Grandchildren? Certain jobs? Trips? When you retire? World events? Inventions? Does your time line stretch beyond your life and way into the future? Go crazy with it!

Mission 25: Modesty and Humility - Tell someone you respect a story about a time in your life when you failed at something important to you. Let yourself be vulnerable. Tell them also about the lessons you learned from your story.

Mission 26: Zest - Dale Carnegie said, "Act enthusiastic and you will be enthusiastic!" Action is the key word today. First draw what you look like when you are enthusiastic. Now, carry that picture around and make sure to make that drawing a reality at least two times today!

Mission 27: Appreciation of Beauty - Find a pattern in nature. It can be the grooves in a tree, waves on the water, anything. Then find a manmade object that contains the same pattern. Which do you find more beautiful and why?

Mission 28: Social Intelligence - Make an effort to meet one new person today, even if it's just to say hello. If you're feeling adventurous, sit with someone different during lunch time.

Mission 29: Gratitude - Create a gratitude calendar of the past week. Write down one thing that happened for each day in the last week for which you are thankful.

Mission 30: Forgiveness - Think of a time you caused someone you care about to be upset or unhappy. Write down three reasons you should forgive yourself for what happened, or three things you might be able to do to make it better.

Mission 31: Open-Mindedness - Before making your next decision, pause and find at least two alternatives to your final decision.

Mission 32: Capacity to Love and Be Loved - Think of a secret you've never told anyone before. Share it with someone you trust. Let them know you are sharing something you have not shared with them before.

Mission 33: Open-Mindedness - Rate yourself on open-mindedness on a scale of 1-10, with 1 being the lowest and 10 being the highest. How can you improve your rating? Why did you give yourself this rating? Do you think those who love you would agree with this rating?

Mission 34: Creativity - If you could have any "superpower," what would it be? What if you could speak and understand every language or breathe underwater? Now give yourself a superhero name. Write three sentences about what your first superhero mission would be like!

Mission 35: Teamwork - Get a small group together and take five minutes together to answer the following question: "Your plane crashed... your group needs to choose the 12 most useful items to survive (you can have anything)... what do you choose?"

Mission 36: Zest - Think about something wonderful in your life. Now jump as high as you can and scream with joy about that great thing!

Mission 37: Social Intelligence - Have all of your conversations today without any distractions. Be completely aware of what someone is saying to you by giving them your full attention.

Mission 38: Capacity to Love and Be Loved - Write a card to someone you love today and give it to them.

Mission 39: Prudence - Take only what you need. Instead of using 10 napkins at lunch, for example, take 1 or 2 or exactly what you need.

Mission 40: Social Intelligence - Examine each person today both on WHAT they say and HOW they say it. Find an example of a match and mismatch between body language and verbal language through your interactions. Look for the subtle clues reflected in eyes, posture, intonation, and more. Write a few sentences about each experience. How can you tell when what someone says matches how they say it?

Mission 41: Fairness - Respond to every statement someone makes to you during the day with more than simple one- or two-word answers. Give everyone a respectable amount of your time and genuine interest.

Mission 42: Curiosity - Research your favorite sport. Learn about its origins, the development of its rules and traditions, and some of its earliest practitioners. How have the rules or the sport changed over time?

Mission 43: Open-Mindedness - Engage in a discussion with someone you consider closed-minded about a given topic. In the course of the discussion, ask questions that force them to defend their position in a structured, thought-out manner.

Mission 44: Modesty and Humility - Tell someone you respect a story about a time in your life when you failed at something important to you. Let yourself be vulnerable. Tell them also about the lessons you learned from your story.

Mission 45: Perseverance - For 30 minutes, be completely silent. Don't move or walk about, and don't go to the bathroom; just focus on staying in one spot. Make as little noise as possible, even if reading and turning pages. Concentrate on your breathing.

Mission 46: Self-Regulation - Make a list of three things that really, really annoy you when other people do them. Choose one from the list, and the next time someone does it, embrace them for their uniqueness rather than resenting them for their action.

Mission 47: Hope - Do something for Mother Nature today; it can be as small as picking up a piece of trash or as large as planting a tree. Encourage a friend to do this with you... spread environmental hope.

Mission 48: Leadership - Good leaders must be good listeners. Listen to a problem a friend is having, and then help them brainstorm some strategies to overcome that problem. Follow up with them to make sure they follow through.

Mission 49: Zest - Create a travel brochure of somewhere you really want to go... use pictures of magazines or draw and color... design something online... make it look GOOD!

Mission 50: Spirituality - Start a dream journal. If you can't remember your dreams (since we don't all remember them every night), record either the first thought you have upon waking or the last you can remember before falling asleep.

Mission 51: Hope - Create a 12-month calendar. For each month, instead of a picture, write down something you've never done that you'd like to accomplish that month.

Mission 52: Humor - Find a comic strip in the paper or a magazine that makes you smile. Cut it out and tape it somewhere unexpected for a friend or loved one to find.

Mission 53: Modesty and Humility - Find an embarrassing picture of yourself (baby pictures are often a good place to start looking) and share it with someone who hasn't previously seen it. Share a laugh at your own expense.

Mission 54: Open-Mindedness - Imagine you live on an island with 5,000 inhabitants. Set up a government and decide how your island will be run. Decide how to divide up the land. How would you feed everyone? Are you the president of a democracy or a dictator? Is this very different from your current government? Why? How can you encourage trust among the people on your island? How do you resolve disputes? Consider what you think is the best way to keep these people happy.

Mission 55: Humor - Create a fun bag for your home. Put anything you want into it, such as books, kazoos, Legos, crayons, Slinkys, bubble wrap, playing cards, etc.... it can be a basketful of items or just one thing, but put it out somewhere for anyone to use.

Mission 56: Honesty - Obtain a plain white T-shirt and a magic marker. Turn the shirt into a label for yourself. Write one word that you feel best describes you on the front and back. Wear the shirt all day.

Mission 57: Love of Learning - Learn a simple phrase in Morse code, something amusing or insightful. Now take what you've learned and teach it to one other person.

Mission 58: Honesty - Find someone who has done something that hurt you and tell them what it was and how it made you feel. Don't ask for an apology (though if they offer, that's great), but let them know how you feel.

Mission 59: Open-Mindedness - Find a piece of art that you don't like. Try to find something beautiful or worthwhile in it. Ask other people their opinions, and listen to what they have to say.

Mission 60: Perspective - Watch TV or a video today with your eyes closed. Allow yourself to only listen. How does this change your perspective?

Mission 61: Bravery - Wear your hair in a new and daring style for the day.

Mission 62: Zest - Greet everyone you meet with a smile and enthusiasm, whether you're happy to see them or not. Many times a greeting is the only interaction we have with someone; do your best to generate a positive impression.

Mission 63: Perseverance - Find a new song you like but have never heard before. Try to memorize all the words in one hour.

Mission 64: Kindness - Watch people's feet as you move through your day. Any time you see someone with an untied shoe, point it out to them so they don't trip.

Mission 65: Open-Mindedness - Find someone who enjoys a sport you don't like or don't understand. Together, either participate in it or watch it on television. Invite your companion to share what they find enjoyable about it.

Mission 66: Curiosity - Look up a word that is unfamiliar to you. More than just the definition of that word, find out where the word comes from (its origin). Now use that word at least two times today.

Mission 67: Creativity - Try to disguise yourself. Your goal is to speak to one person who knows you and have them not recognize you.

Mission 68: Self-Regulation - Pay extra attention to your posture today. Do not slouch the whole day!

Mission 69: Bravery - We all say the sentence, "I've been meaning to do this," or "I've been meaning to tell someone that." Today, be brave and do what you've been putting off. Just do it! How does it make you feel?

Mission 70: Forgiveness - Forgive something or someone who might irritate you today. Do this the second it happens. Make sure you physically shrug your shoulders and say to yourself, "It's no big deal."

Mission 71: Fairness - Search through the news for a story about injustice in the world. Create a list of at least five reasons you feel the situation is unjust. Now, if you could offer a resolution, what would it be? Write it down!

Mission 72: Bravery - Find a food you normally despise eating and eat it today. Try to find a bit of pleasure in the act of eating something you normally dislike.

Mission 73: Perspective - Do a role reversal with a friend or someone you are close with. For an entire hour, become the other person; act like them, speak like them, and think like they do. Have fun with this! What did you gain?

Mission 74: Bravery - We need constant reminders to be brave every day. Give yourself a tangible example of courage. Draw a picture today of courage in action. Don't worry about whether your drawing is good or not! Be brave and dare to be creative! Show your drawing to at least one person.

Mission 75: Teamwork - Making eye contact is sometimes difficult. This activity will develop this skill and cultivate two foundational elements for teamwork-trust and respect. Find someone to work with; stare into your partner's eyes for at least 60 seconds. There may be some giggles at first, as it can feel somewhat awkward during the first try, but as you get the hang of it, it should become easier to make eye contact for prolonged periods of time.

Mission 76: Creativity - Find a partner. Grab a paper and pen. Now, pick a place from your childhood that this partner is not aware of (house, bedroom, park, etc.). Close your eyes and describe this place in as much detail as possible. Use colors, textures, smells, and everything you can to describe this place. As you are speaking, ask the partner to draw exactly what you are saying. Open your eyes! What does it look like? Now, switch!

Mission 77: Creativity - Draw a detailed picture of your life in five years. Choose a venue: work, home, school, and so forth and draw the picture in detail. It doesn't matter if you have no ability to draw. Be as creative as possible with colors.

Mission 78: Humor - What's your favorite joke? Tell it at least three times today.

Mission 79: Honesty - Find someone (friend, family member, classmate) who habitually does something you find annoying or frustrating. Tell them how you feel about what they do.

Mission 80: Modesty and Humility - The word "humility" and the word "human" both come from "humus" or earth. Today as you are walking, tread lightly. Be careful not to step on insects or disturb the ground. Respect your surroundings in your practice of humility.

Mission 81: Creativity - Speak today for at least 15 minutes a day without using the words I, me, my, or mine. What were you restricted from speaking about? How did you get creative to convey your point?

Mission 82: Perseverance - Think of three routine tasks you often avoid doing (such as chores). Go and do at least two of them right now. Now!

Mission 83: Spirituality - Watch the sun rise or set today. As you do, imagine what the day might bring. Now consider someone thousands of miles away watching the same sun rise or set and reflecting on their day. Consider what they might be thinking.

Mission 84: Prudence - Does your backpack have everything you need in it? Double check it and pack extra supplies today!

Mission 85: Curiosity - Think of your dream job or career. Do some research on it. Find out what that job entails, the steps needed to become qualified for it, and some of the challenges that come with it.

Mission 86: Honesty - Have you ever told a secret? Has anyone ever told yours? A broken promise is hard to heal from. Is it OK to expect people to keep their promises? Find or produce an image that represents a promise... something shared between two people.

Mission 87: Perseverance - Reaching a goal inevitably involves obstacles. Although we can't know all of the obstacles in advance, we can anticipate some of them. Doing so gives you a stronger chance of pushing through them should they actually occur. Make a list of some obstacles you might encounter in your current project. Now make a list of how you could conquer them.

Mission 88: Self-Regulation - Make a list of three daily activities you feel you do too much of and three you wish you did more of. Work on balancing the list a little by devoting time from one of the "too much" activities to one on the "not enough" list.

Mission 89: Self-Regulation - Do not respond with anger to anything anyone says or does. Instead, count to ten or try to recite the alphabet backward. Before you're done, ask yourself why you're really angry and if there's a better way to handle your feelings.

Mission 90: Love of Learning - Learn a new type of dance. Whether through a class or video instruction on the Internet, learn the basics of a new dance and find a time and place to try it out.

Mission 91: Forgiveness - Sometimes our loved ones do not pick up on the subtle signs that speak of a need for attention and we feel neglected. Go to someone who has made you feel this way and tell them how you felt, but apologize for feeling bitter about it.

Mission 92: Prudence - Think twice before you speak. Do this at least five times today. See if you can change what you would say by thinking carefully before you speak.

Mission 93: Spirituality - Imagine a perfect version of yourself. Try to be that version for one day. Remember that you cannot control what happens around you, only your reactions to what happens around you.

Mission 94: Appreciation of Beauty - Look at a list of the world flags. Choose the country you think has the most beautiful flag. Try to judge on aesthetics alone, not based on feelings about any of the actual countries.

Mission 95: Forgiveness - Create a small token of forgiveness for someone. It can be a pin, a bookmark, or just a card, but give it to someone you feel you need to forgive and ask that they, in turn, pass it to someone they need to forgive for something, and so on.

Mission 96: Modesty and Humility - Enter a group situation in which you let everyone speak and contribute more than you do. Encourage the group to speak and contribute more by asking questions.

Mission 97: Appreciation of Beauty - Appreciate something in nature with all of your senses. Find a leaf or something that you think is beautiful and spend time with this wonder using touch, sight, smell, sound, and yes--even taste (if it makes sense)! Notice how you may or may not use all of your senses when it comes to your appreciation of beauty.

Mission 98: Open-Mindedness - Let someone else pick out the clothes you are going to wear today. Without judgment, wear them!

Mission 99: Curiosity - We are so often afraid to question what someone tells us. Make it a point today to ask people why they are asking you to do something or why they are doing what they are doing. Being curious is a wonderful way to learn something new.

Answers: What's Right with This Picture?

Some possible strengths are displayed in the picture below. You might see different strengths based on what you feel is happening in the image. Be creative in finding other strengths in the scene below!

Answers: Strength Word Search

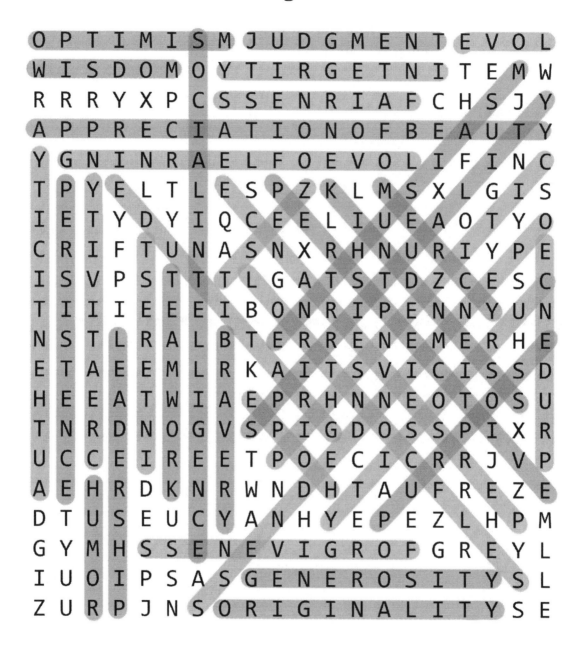

Answers: Strengths Crossword Puzzle

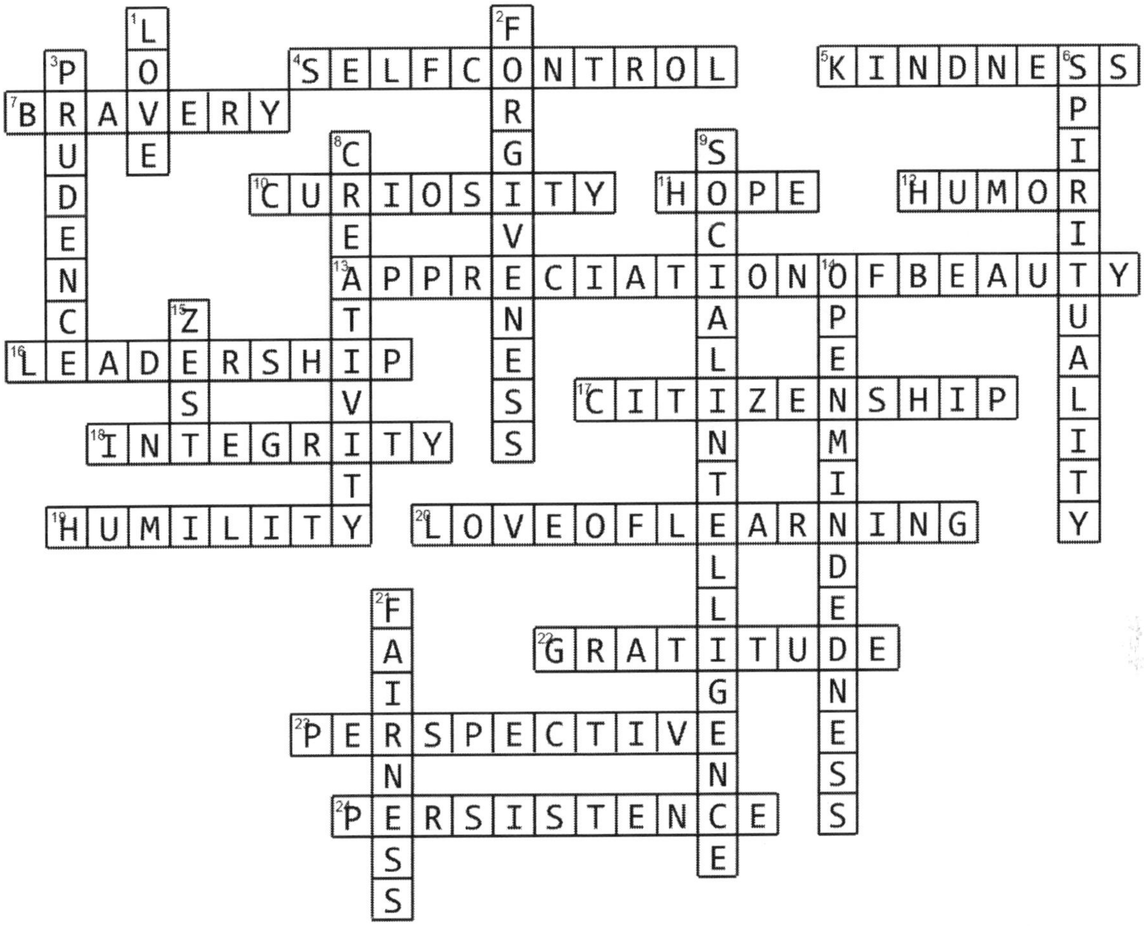
1 LOVE
2 FORGIVENESS
3 PRUDENCE
4 SELFCONTROL
5 KINDNESS
6 SPIRITUALITY
7 BRAVERY
8 CREATIVITY
9 SOCIALINTELLIGENCE
10 CURIOSITY
11 HOPE
12 HUMOR
13 APPRECIATIONOFBEAUTY
14 OPENMINDEDNESS
15 ZEST
16 LEADERSHIP
17 CITIZENSHIP
18 INTEGRITY
19 HUMILITY
20 LOVEOFLEARNING
21 FAIRNESS
22 GRATITUDE
23 PERSPECTIVE
24 PERSISTENCE

Across:

4. Controlling what you feel and do; being disciplined; controlling your appetites and emotions. (Answer: Self-Control)

5. Performing good deeds for others. (Answer: Kindness)

7. Taking on danger, challenges, difficulty, or pain; acting on your beliefs even if they're not popular. (Answer: Bravery)

10. Taking an interest in experiences; exploring and discovering new things. (Answer: Curiosity)

11. Expecting the best in the future and working to achieve it. (Answer: Hope)

12. Liking to laugh and tease; bringing smiles to other people; seeing the lighter side of things. (Answer: Humor)

13. Valuing something awe-inspiring, beautiful, excellent. (Answer: Appreciation of Beauty)

16. Encouraging a group to get things done while maintaining good relationships with everyone in the group. (Answer: Leadership)

17. Working well as a member of a group or team; showing that you are a responsible member of a community. (Answer: Citizenship)

18. Being yourself; taking responsibility for your feelings and actions. (Answer: Integrity)

19. Letting your accomplishments speak for themselves. (Answer: Humility)

20. Having fun in mastering new skills. (Answer: Love of Learning)

22. Being thankful for good things that happen; taking time to express thanks. (Answer: Gratitude)

23. Having ways of looking at the world that make sense to yourself and others. (Answer: Perspective)

24. Finishing what you start; not giving up when faced with obstacles. (Answer: Persistence)

Down:

1. A feeling of strong affection for someone or something. (Answer: Love)

2. Giving people a second chance; not being vengeful. (Answer: Forgiveness)

3. Being careful about your choices; not taking unnecessary risks; not saying or doing things that you might later regret. (Answer: Prudence)

6. Having clear beliefs about a higher purpose, the meaning of life, the meaning of the universe. (Answer: Spirituality)

8. Finding new ways to do or think about things. (Answer: Creativity)

9. Being aware of the motives and feelings of other people and yourself. (Answer: Social Intelligence)

14. Being willing to consider different ideas or opinions. (Answer: Open-Mindedness)

15. Approaching life with excitement and energy; feeling alive and activated. (Answer: Zest)

21. Treating all people the same. (Answer: Fairness)

References

The VIA Classification

The VIA classification is the fruit of a multiyear project in which 55 top social scientists asked the following question: What is best about humans? Over three years, these scientists researched the world's major writings on religion, philosophy, organizational studies, youth development, psychiatry, and psychology, among others, to seek out the virtues and strengths valued across cultures and time. The goal was for this group to leave no stone unturned in order to produce an exhaustive list of character strengths. In order to avoid redundancies and narrow the list, the group made sure each strength followed certain criteria:

Each character strength...

- is ubiquitous or widely recognized across cultures

- is fulfilling or contributes to individual fulfillment, satisfaction, and happiness

- is morally valued or valued on its own and not for any outcome it may produce

- does not diminish others or elevates others who see it in action

- has an opposite or has obvious antonyms that are negative

- is trait-like or exhibits patterns that are generally stable over time

- is measurable or has been successfully measured by researchers

- is distinct or is not redundant with other strengths

- has paragons or individuals who are exemplars of the strength

- has prodigies or is shown precociously in some youth

- can be selectively absent or missing in some individuals altogether

- has enabling institutions or is a deliberate goal of society

The result of all of this work is the VIA classification, or the list of 6 core virtues and the 24 character strengths categorized within them.

Check it out:

Wisdom and Knowledge - Cognitive strengths that entail the acquisition and use of knowledge.

- Creativity [originality, ingenuity]: Thinking of novel and productive ways to conceptualize and do things; includes artistic achievement but is not limited to it.

- Curiosity [interest, novelty-seeking, openness to experience]: Taking an interest in ongoing experience for its own sake; finding subjects and topics fascinating; exploring and discovering.

- Judgment [critical thinking]: Thinking things through and examining them from all sides; not jumping to conclusions; being able to change one's mind in light of evidence; weighing all evidence fairly.

- Love of Learning: Mastering new skills, topics, and bodies of knowledge, whether on one's own or formally; obviously related to the strength of curiosity but goes beyond it to describe the tendency to add systematically to what one knows.

- Perspective [wisdom]: Being able to provide wise counsel to others; having ways of looking at the world that make sense to oneself and to other people.

Courage - Emotional strengths that involve the exercise of will to accomplish goals in the face of opposition, external or internal.

- Bravery [valor]: Not shrinking from threat, challenge, difficulty, or pain; speaking up for what is right even if there is opposition; acting on convictions even if unpopular; includes physical bravery but is not limited to it.

- Perseverance [persistence, industriousness]: Finishing what one starts; persisting in a course of action in spite of obstacles; "getting it out the door"; taking pleasure in completing tasks.

- Honesty [authenticity, integrity]: Speaking the truth but more broadly presenting oneself in a genuine way and acting in a sincere way; being without pretense; taking responsibility for one's feelings and actions.

- Zest [vitality, enthusiasm, vigor, energy]: Approaching life with excitement and energy; not doing things halfway or halfheartedly; living life as an adventure; feeling alive and activated.

Humanity - Interpersonal strengths that involve tending and befriending others.

- Love: Valuing close relations with others, in particular those in which sharing and caring are reciprocated; being close to people.

- Kindness [generosity, nurturance, care, compassion, altruistic love, "niceness"]: Doing favors and good deeds for others; helping them; taking care of them.

- Social Intelligence [emotional intelligence, personal intelligence]: Being aware of the motives and feelings of other people and oneself; knowing what to do to fit into different social situations; knowing what makes other people tick.

Justice - Civic strengths that underlie healthy community life.

- Teamwork [citizenship, social responsibility, loyalty]: Working well as a member of a group or team; being loyal to the group; doing one's share.

- Fairness: Treating all people the same according to notions of fairness and justice; not letting personal feelings bias decisions about others; giving everyone a fair chance.

- Leadership: Encouraging a group of which one is a member to get things done, and at the same time maintaining good relations within the group; organizing group activities and seeing that they happen.

Temperance - Strengths that protect against excess.

- Forgiveness: Forgiving those who have done wrong; accepting the shortcomings of others; giving people a second chance; not being vengeful.

- Humility: Letting one's accomplishments speak for themselves; not regarding oneself as more special than one is.

- Prudence: Being careful about one's choices; not taking undue risks; not saying or doing things that might later be regretted.

- Self-Regulation [self-control]: Regulating what one feels and does; being disciplined; controlling one's appetites and emotions.

Transcendence - Strengths that forge connections to the larger universe and provide meaning.

- Appreciation of Beauty and Excellence [awe, wonder, elevation]: Noticing and appreciating beauty, excellence, and/or skilled performance in various domains of life, from nature to art to mathematics to science to everyday experience.

- Gratitude: Being aware of and thankful for the good things that happen; taking time to express thanks.

- Hope [optimism, future-mindedness, future orientation]: Expecting the best in the future and working to achieve it; believing that a good future is something that can be brought about.

- Humor [playfulness]: Liking to laugh and tease; bringing smiles to other people; seeing the light side; making (not necessarily telling) jokes.

- Spirituality [faith, purpose]: Having coherent beliefs about the higher purpose and meaning of the universe; knowing where one fits within the larger scheme; having beliefs about the meaning of life that shape conduct and provide comfort.

The VIA Classification was reprinted with permission. Copyright 2004-2013 VIA® Institute on Character; All rights reserved.

Researched Benefits

Are there benefits to teaching our youth about character strengths? You betcha! Check out some of the research:

- In a longitudinal study of adolescents' transition to middle school, intellectual and temperance strengths predicted school performance and achievement, interpersonal strengths related to school social functioning, and temperance and transcendence strengths predicted well-being (Shoshani & Slone, 2012).

- In a study of children's adjustment to first grade, parents' intellectual, interpersonal, and temperance strengths related to their child's school adjustment, while the children's intellectual, interpersonal, temperance, and transcendence strengths related to first-grade adjustment (Shoshani & Ilanit Aviv, 2012).

- In a study of adolescents' character strengths and career/vocational interests, intellectual strengths were related to investigative and artistic career interests, transcendence and other-oriented strengths were related to social career interests, and leadership strengths were associated with enterprising career interests (Proyer, Sidler, Weber, & Ruch, 2012).

- In a study of adolescent romantic relationships, honesty, humor, and love were the most preferred character strengths in an ideal partner (Weber & Ruch, 2012a).

- Character strengths of the mind (e.g., self-regulation, perseverance, love of learning) were predictive of school success (Weber & Ruch, 2012b).

- In a study of the VIA Youth Survey, five strengths factors emerged and were independently associated with well-being and happiness (Toner, Haslam, Robinson, & Williams, 2012).

- A study of 319 adolescent students between the ages of 12-14 were divided into two groups in which 2/3 received character strength-building activities and strengths challenges within the school curriculum (called Strengths Gym), and 1/3 did not; those who participated in strengths experienced increased in life satisfaction compared to the controls (Proctor et al., 2011).

- Among high school students, other-oriented strengths (e.g., kindness, teamwork) predicted fewer depression symptoms while transcendence strengths (e.g., spirituality) predicted greater life satisfaction (Gillham et al., 2011).

- Positive education programming which heavily involves character strengths assessment and intervention led to improved student school skills and greater student enjoyment and engagement in school (e.g., improved curiosity, love of learning, and creativity; Seligman et al., 2009).

- The most prevalent character strengths in very young children are love, kindness, creativity, curiosity, and humor (Park & Peterson, 2006a).

- When compared with U.S. adults, youth from the U.S. are higher on the character strengths of hope, teamwork, and zest and adults are higher on appreciation of beauty & excellence, honesty, leadership, open-mindedness (Park & Peterson, 2006b).

- Convergence of strengths between parents and child are modest except for spirituality where it is substantial (Peterson & Seligman, 2004)

- Character strengths with a developmental trajectory (least common in youth and increase over time through cognitive maturation) are appreciation of beauty & excellence, forgiveness, modesty, open-mindedness (Park & Peterson, 2006a; 2006b).

- Focus groups with 459 high school students from 20 high schools found that students largely believe the 24 VIA strengths are acquired and that the strengths develop through ongoing experience, the students cited minimal character strength role models, and they particularly valued the strengths of love of learning, perspective, love, social intelligence, leadership, and spirituality (Steen, Kachorek, & Peterson, 2003).

www.viacharacter.org

Academic References

The ideas in this book have been supported by the following research:

Baumeister, R. F., Bratslavsky, E., Finkenauer, C., & Vohs, K. D. (2001). Bad is stronger than good. Review of General Psychology, 5(4), 323-370.

Fredrickson, B. (2009). *Positivity.* New York: Crown Publishers.

Park, N., & Peterson, C. (2009). Character strengths: Research and practice. Journal of College and Character, 10(4), np.

Peterson, C., & Seligman, M. E. (2004). *Character strengths and virtues: a handbook and classification.* New York: Oxford University Press/Washington, DC: American Psychological Association

Peterson, C. (2006). *A primer in positive psychology.* New York: Oxford University Press.

Seligman, M. E. (2002). *Authentic happiness: using the new positive psychology to realize your potential for lasting fulfillment.* New York: Free Press.

Seligman, M. E. P., Steen, T. A., Park, N., & Peterson, C. (2005). Positive psychology progress: Empirical validation of interventions. *American Psychologist, 60,* 410-421.

The references supporting the research found in this reference section:

Gillham, J., Adams-Deutsch, Z., Werner, J., Reivich, K., Coulter-Heindl, V., Linkins, M., Winder, B., Peterson, C., Park, N., Abenavoli, R., Contero, A., & Seligman, M. E. P. (2011). Character strengths predict subjective well-being during adolescence. *Journal of Positive Psychology, 6*(1), 31-44.

Park, N., & Peterson, C. (2006a). Character strengths and happiness among young children: Content analysis of parental descriptions.*Journal of Happiness Studies, 7,* 323-341.

Park, N., & Peterson, C. (2006b). Moral competence and character strengths among adolescents: The development and validation of the Values in Action Inventory of Strengths for Youth. *Journal of Adolescence, 29,* 891-905.

Park, N., & Peterson, C. (2009a). Character strengths: Research and practice. *Journal of College and Character, 10*(4), np.

Park, N., & Peterson, C. (2009b). Strengths of character in schools. In R. Gilman, E. S. Huebner, & M. J. Furlong (Eds.), *Handbook of positive psychology in schools* (pp. 65-76). New York: Routledge.

Park, N., Peterson, C., & Seligman, M. E. P. (2004). Strengths of character and well-being. *Journal of Social & Clinical Psychology, 23*, 603-619.

Proctor, C., Tsukayama, E., Wood, A., M., Maltby, J., Fox Eades, J., & Linley, P. A. (2011). Strengths gym: The impact of a character strengths-based intervention on the life satisfaction and well-being of adolescents. *Journal of Positive Psychology, 6*(5), 377-388.

Proyer, R. T., Sidler, N., Weber, M., & Ruch, W. (2012). A multi-method approach to studying the relationship between character strengths and vocational interests in adolescents. *International Journal for Educational and Vocational Guidance, 12*(2), 141-157.

Seligman, M. E. P., Ernst, R. M., Gillham, J., Reivich, K., & Linkins, M. (2009). Positive education: Positive psychology and classroom interventions. *Oxford Review of Education, 35*(3), 293-311.

Shoshani, A., & Ilanit Aviv, I. (2012). The pillars of strength for first-grade adjustment - Parental and children's character strengths and the transition to elementary school. *Journal of Positive Psychology, 7*(4), 315-326.

Shoshani, A., & Slone, M. (2012). Middle school transition from the strengths perspective: Young adolescents' character strengths, subjective well-being, and school adjustment. *Journal of Happiness Studies.*

Steen, T. A., Kachorek, L. V., & Peterson, C. (2003). Character strengths among youth. *Journal of Youth & Adolescence, 32*(1), 5-16.

Toner, E., Haslam, N., Robinson, J., & Williams, P. (2012). Character strengths and wellbeing in adolescence: Structure and correlates of the Values in Action Inventory of Strengths for Children. *Personality and Individual Differences, 52*(5), 637-642.

Weber, M., & Ruch, W. (2012a). The role of character strengths in adolescent romantic relationships: An initial study on partner selection and mates' life satisfaction. *Journal of Adolescence.*

Weber, M., & Ruch, W. (2012b). The role of a good character in 12-year-old school children: Do character strengths matter in the classroom? *Child Indicators Research, 5*(2), 317-334.

About the Author

My name is Renee Jain (pronounced Ree-knee Jane) and many of the stories within GoStrengths! and GoZen! programs are based on the challenges I faced while growing up. You see, I was raised by loving and supportive parents and had a pretty decent life, but I never learned to cope with adversity—not properly, at least. I was the queen of exaggeration... little molehills in my life regularly blew up into mountains of pain and sorrow. I often suffered in silence clutching onto my motto, "No one gets it."

I learned much later in life that people do indeed understand what kids go through when they feel anxious, depressed, misunderstood, or just plain stressed out. I learned there are effective methods to cope with problems and increase one's resilience. I also discovered that beyond the capacity to survive, it is possible to learn how to thrive. Happiness is a skill which can be practiced, and life can offer deep meaning, purpose, and joy. With the help of Neutrino, I hope to take the lessons I have gleaned through my personal and professional experience and pass them on to as many other humanoids as possible.

I invite you to join me on my journey. **Together we can change the lives of the next generation by equipping them with skills of happiness and resilience—skills which will propel them toward every measure of success possible. Get in touch with me at *reneejain.com*. I'd love to hear from you!**

Some professional stuff:

Renee is one of less than 300 people in the world to earn her Master's degree in Positive Psychology—the scientific study of optimal human functioning—from the University of Pennsylvania. Renee has been personally mentored and trained by some of the top depression prevention experts in the world. A gifted life coach, she has coached over 5,000 clients in the science of resilience.

The Fun Doesn't Stop Here!

Having fun with strengths?

Want to learn more about strengths and get more fun activities? Check out the GoStrengths! animated social and emotional learning tools and programs at *www.gostrengths.com*!

Check out our other work!

Check out the awesome workbook from our sister site GoZen!, which is dedicated to the anxiety relief of all youthlings.

http://bit.ly/gozenwkbk

Join us on these amazing humanoid social sites:

Chat with us on Facebook: *http://www.facebook.com/askneutrino*

Hook up with us on Twitter: *http://www.twitter.com/askneutrino*

Get free videos for our programs here: *http://www.gostrengths.com*

PLEASE help us spread the word!!!

We are looking to spread the word. If you think this workbook is valuable, please help us reach as many humanoids as possible by writing a review. Thank you—see you very soon!

Made in the USA
San Bernardino, CA
20 February 2018